Steve Jobs

Technology Innovator *and* Apple Genius

Steve Jobs

Technology Innovator *and* Apple Genius

Matt Doeden

Lerner Publications Company • Minneapolis

Lerner Publications Company
A division of Lerner Publishing Group, Inc.
241 First Avenue North
Minneapolis, MN U.S.A. 55401

Website address: www.lernerbooks.com

Library of Congress Cataloging-in-Publication Data

Doeden, Matt.
    Steve Jobs : technology innovator and Apple genius / by Matt Doeden.
        p.   cm. — (Gateway biographies)
    Includes bibliographical references and index.
    ISBN 978-1-4677-0215-7 (lib. bdg. : alk. paper)
    1. Jobs, Steve, 1955–2011—Juvenile literature. 2. Computer engineers—United States—Biography—Juvenile literature. 3. Inventors—United States—Biography—Juvenile literature. 4. Businesspeople—United States—Biography—Juvenile literature. 5. Apple Computer, Inc.—Juvenile literature. I. Title.
    QA76.2.J63D64 2012
    338.7′61004092—dc23 [B]   2011046268

Manufactured in the United States of America
1 – DP – 12/31/11

The images in this book are used with the permission of: © Justin Sullivan/Getty Images, pp. 2, 6, 8, 37; Seth Poppel Yearbook Library, p. 11; © Apic/Hulton Archive/Getty Images, p. 12; © Mickey Pfleger/Time & Life Pictures/Getty Images, p. 13; © DPA/Landov, pp. 17, 23; © SiliconValleyStock/Alamy, p. 18; © Kim Kulish/CORBIS, p. 19; © Owen Franken/CORBIS, p. 20; © Tom Munnecke/Hulton Archive/Getty Images, p. 21; © Marilyn K. Yee/New York Times/Archive Photos/Getty Images, p. 27; © Blake Sell/Reuters/Landov, p. 28; © Brian Ach/WireImage/Getty Images, p. 29; © Buena Vista Pictures/Everett Collection, p. 30; © Gabe Palacio/Getty Images, p. 32; © Randall Quan/Bloomberg via Getty Images, p. 33; © David Paul Morris/Getty Images, p. 35; © Ian Gavan/Stringer/Getty Images, p. 36; © Joe Raedle/Getty Images, p. 38; © Kevork Djansezian/Getty Images, p. 39.
Front cover: Reuters/Robert Galbraith.

Main body text set is Rotif Serif Std 55 Regular 14/17
Typeface provided by Agfa

Contents

Steve Jobs unveils the iPad on January 27, 2010.

On January 27, 2010, Apple chief executive officer (CEO) Steve Jobs stepped calmly onto a stage in San Francisco, California. Jobs wore his trademark jeans and black turtleneck as he addressed an enthusiastic crowd of eight hundred Apple employees, business partners, and journalists.

Everyone was there to see Jobs's latest, greatest creation—the iPad. Jobs had already reached a near-godlike status among technology buffs. He'd introduced the world to gadgets from the Macintosh computer to the iPod to the iPhone. Everything he touched seemed to turn to gold, and rumors about the iPad had been circulating for months.

As Jobs showed off the newest piece of Apple wizardry, some were cautious. The iPad was a tablet computer—a slim, flat, touch-screen computer without a dedicated keyboard. Tablets had been around for decades. Consumers had rejected them time and again. Why would the iPad be any different? the skeptics wondered.

Others knew why. The iPad would succeed because it was a creation of Steve Jobs. Jobs wasn't an engineer

Jobs explores and demonstrates the features of the iPad as he speaks at an Apple special event.

or a programmer. He was a man who understood technology and understood how people wanted to use it. For Jobs, everything was about the user experience. And the iPad was no exception. Anyone could pick one up and understand instantly how to use it. The elegant, simple design was inviting and, some argued, almost addictive.

"[The iPad is] so much more intimate than a laptop, and it's so much more capable than a smartphone with its gorgeous screen," Jobs told the crowd. "It's phenomenal to hold the Internet in your hands."

Once again, Jobs was correct. The iPad was a hit, and soon a wave of copycat tablets was flooding the market. It was the perfect example of Jobs's genius. He took a product that had been around for decades and put his own spin on it. Then he turned it into a product that suddenly everyone seemed to want to own. Once again, Jobs and Apple had struck gold. And once again, Jobs had turned the computer industry on its ear.

Finding a Family

Steven Paul Jobs was born on February 24, 1955, in San Francisco, California. His birth parents, Joanne Schieble and Abdulfattah "John" Jandali, were graduate students at the University of Wisconsin. Joanne feared that her family would reject a baby born out of wedlock. So she chose to give up her unnamed child for adoption.

Baby Steve wasn't without a family for long, however. Paul and Clara Jobs had been married for nine years and wanted a family. Clara was unable to become pregnant, so the couple found little Steve, adopted him, and gave him his name. Three years later, the couple adopted a daughter, Patty. The family settled in Santa Clara County, south of San Francisco.

From the beginning, Paul and Clara were honest and open with Steve about where he came from. Once, when Steve was about seven years old, a discussion with a neighbor girl upset him. She told him that his birth parents hadn't wanted him. Steve recalled how Paul and Clara eased his concern. "I remember running into the house, crying. And my parents said, 'No, you have to understand.' They were very serious and looked me straight in the eye. They said, 'We specifically picked you out.' Both of my parents said that and repeated it slowly for me. And they put an emphasis on every word in that sentence."

Clara and Paul gave Steve a happy and enriching childhood. Clara knew that her son was bright, and she taught Steve to read before he even started school. Paul, a machinist by trade, was very handy. In his spare time, he loved to work on cars. He bought old cars, restored them, and then sold them for a profit. The extra money went into a college fund for Steve and Patty. Paul also gave Steve a little workbench and tools so he could work on projects of his own. Steve was especially captivated by electronics. "[My father] spent a lot of time with me, teaching me how to build things, how to take things apart, put things back together," Steve recalled.

Young Steve proved to be a bit of a challenge in school. His test scores were always very high. But his attention often wandered. He didn't like to study. He could be a troublemaker and a prankster. But Steve's fourth-grade teacher, Imogene "Teddy" Hill, inspired a love of learning in young Steve. He suddenly became an excellent, focused student. He wanted to learn and soaked up information quickly. With his newfound sense of focus, Steve was ready to excel.

Whiz Kid

At the end of fourth grade, Steve was testing at the level of a tenth grader. So the school and his parents agreed that he would skip a grade. They thought that putting Steve in sixth grade would give him more of a challenge. They were right—but the challenges Steve faced weren't quite what they had hoped for. Suddenly surrounded by older kids, Steve felt out of place. He was awkward and frequently bullied. He hated school and threatened to quit. It got so bad that the Jobs family moved just so Steve could attend a different school. The switch worked, and he made it to Homestead High School.

Meanwhile, Steve's fascination with electronics continued. In high school, he joined the Hewlett-Packard Explorers Club. The club included about fifteen students who shared his interest in engineering and elec-tronics. Once an engineer with the Hewlett-Packard company showed Steve one of the computers the company was developing.

Jobs in his high school senior portrait

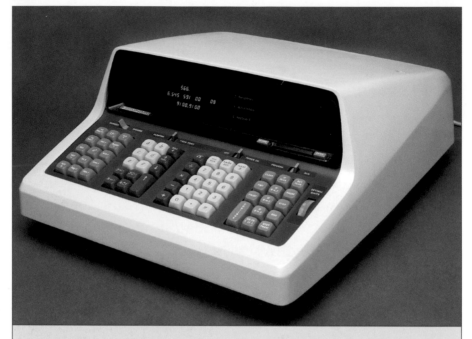

Hewlett-Packard's 9100A computer—an early desktop machine that helped to spark Jobs's passion for computers

"It was called the 9100A," Steve recalled. "It was a glorified calculator but also really the first desktop computer. It was huge, maybe forty pounds [18 kilograms], but it was a beauty of a thing. I fell in love with it."

Steve wanted some spare computer parts for a project he was working on. So he opened up a phone book and found the listing for William Packard—the CEO of Hewlett-Packard. Steve made the call, and the two ended up chatting. Packard got Steve the spare parts he needed. Packard was so impressed with Steve that he also gave him a summer job assembling computer parts.

Steve hung out as much as he could with the engineers, soaking in everything they told him.

Around this time, Steve met fellow computer enthusiast Steve Wozniak. Wozniak was an engineering whiz who had recently dropped out of the University of California at Berkeley. He loved to build electronic gadgets. The two Steves quickly hit it off, despite the fact that Wozniak was four years older than Jobs. Together, they built a blue box—a device used to hack into phone lines so the hacker could make free long-distance calls. Since they didn't have anyone they really wanted to call, they used the box to make prank calls—including one to the pope in Italy! According to Jobs, the pair built and sold about one hundred of the machines.

"If it hadn't been for the blue boxes, there wouldn't have been an Apple," Jobs later said. "Woz and I learned how to work together, and we gained the confidence that we could solve technical problems and actually put something into production."

Steve Wozniak—nicknamed Woz—around 1985

Things were changing quickly for Steve. He had his first girlfriend, Chrisann Brennan. He began smoking marijuana. By his senior year, he was experimenting with harder drugs such as LSD. Steve's father once caught him with drugs. But despite a rare fight between the two, Steve refused to stop. His drug use continued after he graduated from Homestead High School in 1972. Steve headed north to Portland, Oregon, where he briefly attended Reed College. But college life didn't suit Steve, and he soon dropped out. He was ready to start a career in computers.

Working Man

Steve Jobs was always a hard worker. In addition to his job at Hewlett-Packard, he had his own paper route. He saved his money, and by the age of fifteen, he was able to buy his own car—a Nash Metropolitan. But that wasn't good enough for Steve. He wanted a *cool* car. So he kept saving for another year until he could trade in the Nash for a red Fiat 850 Coupe. "My dad helped me buy and inspect it," Steve recalled. "The satisfaction of getting paid and saving up for something, that was very exciting."

Core of an Idea

Even after Jobs dropped out of Reed College, he continued sitting in on classes. He'd sleep on friends' floors and get free meals at a local Hindu temple. One of the classes Jobs sat in on was in calligraphy (decorative handwriting). Something about the artistic letters spoke to Jobs. The style stood out in stark contrast to the blocky, dull font (style of letters and numbers) used in the computer world.

In 1974 Jobs took a job designing video games for Atari. According to his boss, Al Alcorn, Jobs just showed up one day at the Atari office in sandals and demanded to be hired. "I saw something in him," Alcorn said. "He was very intelligent, enthusiastic, excited about tech." Jobs worked on the circuit board for a game called *Breakout*. There, he was reunited with his old Hewlett-Packard friend Steve Wozniak. After Jobs took a trip to India that summer, the two began to get serious about the idea of starting their own company. They both attended meetings of the Homebrew Computer Club—a club for people who were interested in building home-made computers.

In 1975 the first personal computer, the Altair, was released. It wasn't much of a computer. It didn't even come assembled and couldn't do much. But its very existence inspired Jobs and Wozniak. What if they could build a computer that was easy to use and actually *did* something? Wozniak took the lead. He imagined a computer in which a monitor, a keyboard, and a processor were all part

Searching for Meaning

In the summer of 1974, Jobs traveled to India with his friend Daniel Kottke. Jobs had grown very interested in Asian religions, including Hinduism and Zen Buddhism. The main reason for his trip was to meet a Hindu guru (holy man) called Neem Karoli Baba. Jobs was disappointed to find that the guru had died, however. So Jobs spent his time backpacking through India and experimenting with LSD and other drugs. Wozniak later described the change in Jobs upon his return to the United States. "Steve was into everything hippy," said Wozniak. "He ran around shouting 'free love, man' and eating seeds."

of the same unit. He got the parts he needed, wrote the code, and managed to produce a sort of working prototype (first version). Jobs was impressed. He suggested adding memory to the machine for data storage. He also brought a sense of business to the work, convincing Wozniak to sell the final product and using his natural talent for wheeling and dealing to find cheap parts to build more. And just like that, Jobs and Wozniak were on their way.

To start their company, Jobs and Wozniak needed money. So Wozniak sold his high-end scientific calculator for $500. Jobs sold his car for $1,500. They pooled the money and dug in, building computers. All they needed was a company name. Jobs, by this time a vegetarian, often focused on eating only one food or group of foods for a long period of time. At the time, Jobs was eating mainly fruit. After a visit to an apple orchard, he suggested the name the company would take: Apple Computers.

Jobs *(left)* and Wozniak in 1976, working in Jobs's parents' garage

Jobs made the company's first sale, to a small computer store called the Byte Shop. They had to produce fifty Apple I circuit boards to fill the order. Jobs and Wozniak enlisted any help they could get and got to work in the Jobses' garage. Even Jobs's very pregnant sister, Patty, pitched in. Paul Jobs was happy to move his used cars out of the garage, while Clara allowed her house to be taken over by the young computer-builders. It was a total team effort, and they managed to fill the order and claim their first real income—$15,000. Apple Computers was off and running.

Jobs's parents' house, where Jobs and Wozniak started Apple Computers

This Apple I—which consisted of a circuit board and a kit of parts for users to assemble—is on display at the Computer History Museum in Mountain View, California.

Taking Off

After their big score with the Byte Shop, Apple had enough money to build more than one hundred computers. Jobs hit the streets, selling to computer enthusiasts as well as retail outlets. Meanwhile, Wozniak got to work building the next version of the Apple. Their efforts had begun to gain them some notice in the small computer-enthusiast community. The July 1976 issue of *Interface*, a hobbyist magazine, featured a story on Jobs, Wozniak, and Apple. Later that year, they attended a computer conference. While the Apple I was the star of the show in terms of what it could do, other personal computers (PCs) looked more polished and professional. Jobs realized that a computer's outer look was almost as important as what it could do. He asked a designer to come up with an elegant case of molded plastic that could house a computer. It was a big expense, but one Jobs felt was needed. This idea of giving technology an appealing outer look would drive Apple for the next several decades. ·

Wozniak's next creation, the Apple II, stood head and shoulders above the Apple I. Of course, the more advanced machine was also more costly to make. It fell to Jobs to find parts cheaply and to convince people to pay the hefty price tag that came with the new-and-improved machine.

Still, not everyone appreciated Jobs's contributions to the company. Wozniak's father once confronted Jobs, saying he didn't deserve to own half the company. The Apple I

The Apple II was a big step up from the Apple I. It came ready to use and housed in a carefully crafted plastic case.

and II, after all, were Wozniak's creations. Jobs talked to his friend about his father's concerns. He even offered to give up his share of the company. But Wozniak knew that he needed Jobs. And so the partnership lived on. However, all was not well between the two. Their ideas for Apple began to go in different directions. Wozniak wanted to build a machine for the computer enthusiast. Jobs wanted to build a computer for the masses. Disagreements over design became increasingly common.

Jobs brought in investor and marketing specialist Mike Markkula, giving him a share of the company in exchange for $250,000 in capital to build the Apple II. Markkula, who had far more business experience than either Jobs or Wozniak, quickly started making his mark on the company. He convinced Jobs and Wozniak to always focus on the customer's experience when building their product. He encouraged the two former computer hackers to think in terms of a person who knew little about computers—a key to expanding

Mike Markkula poses for a photo with the Apple II.

their business. Markkula and Jobs worked well together. Some outsiders described Markkula as almost a father figure to the young Jobs.

Jobs unveiled the Apple II at the West Coast Computer Faire in San Francisco in April 1977. It was an instant hit. Word of Apple's new home computer began to spread, and orders came in faster and faster. Profits came rolling in. The Apple II was a sensation in the computer world. Its slick packaging and friendly interface (the way a computer user interacts with a computer) had redefined the home computer industry. It was a machine that could fit into almost any home. One didn't have to be a computer expert to figure out how to use it. The Apple II would go on to sell more than six million units. Apple was growing by leaps and bounds. But change was on the horizon.

Struggling with Success

Jobs, still just twenty-two years old, found himself at the head of one of the most successful up-and-coming computer companies in the world. He wasn't prepared for the role. Markkula recalled that Jobs had little tolerance for anything less than perfection. "He became increasingly tyrannical and sharp in his criticism," Markkula said. Jobs was confrontational, self-centered, and often petty, even throwing a tantrum when the company adopted badges and Jobs got badge No. 2 while Wozniak got No. 1.

Wozniak and Jobs stand together in 1978. The young men had different ideas about how Apple should be run.

Markkula and Wozniak agreed that they needed someone to help control Jobs's growing ego. Markkula hired a former coworker, Mike Scott, to serve as Apple's president. One of Scott's main jobs was to manage the increasingly unpopular Jobs. But the two clashed, and Jobs chafed under Scott's management.

Jobs's outbursts weighed heavily on Wozniak. "Steve was too tough on people," Wozniak said. "I wanted our company to feel like a family where we all had fun and shared whatever we made." Meanwhile, Jobs called Wozniak childish and felt that he didn't have any business sense. Many close to Jobs also believed that he felt jealous of Wozniak, who got most of the credit for Apple's success. For all these reasons, the friendship between the two was suffering.

Jobs's personal life was also in a state of disarray. He had reconnected with his now-former girlfriend Chrisann Brennan. And by late 1977, Brennan was pregnant. But Jobs refused to deal with the situation, going so far at times as to deny that he was the father. Brennan gave birth to a daughter on May 17, 1978. Jobs visited Brennan and his daughter and helped pick out a name, Lisa Nicole Brennan. Beyond that, Jobs refused to have much of anything to do with his daughter. He was twenty-three years old—the same age his birth parents had been when they'd given him up for adoption. Jobs later admitted regret over how he'd dealt with the situation. "I wish I had handled it differently," he said. "I could not see myself as a father then, so I didn't face up to it. . . . If I could do it over, I would do a better job."

Despite Jobs's often erratic behavior, Apple was doing better than ever. Sales of the Apple II were soaring. The company was growing and was recognized as one of the leaders in the industry. In 1980 Apple went public. That means the company was divided into shares, which were then sold to investors. At the start of the first day, each share was valued at $22. By the day's end, their worth had climbed to $29. Jobs's cut of that was in the neighborhood of $250 million. At the age of twenty-five, he was already a very rich man.

Dark Days

By 1981 Jobs knew that the Apple II's time was nearing an end. Apple needed a new design to stay at the forefront of the home computer industry. But that same year, Wozniak was involved in an airplane crash. Wozniak survived but left Apple so that he could recover. Wozniak also married around this time. (He would eventually return to Apple in 1983 but in a greatly diminished role.) The genius behind the Apple II was gone. It fell to Jobs to come up with the company's next creation.

That creation was the Apple III. Jobs insisted that the Apple III not come with a noisy fan inside it, as was typical for computers at that time. He instead wanted the computer's case to carry away the heat generated by the computer. But the design was flawed. The Apple III constantly overheated. Apple had to recall thousands of computers. This did tremendous damage to Apple's reputation.

The Apple III may have been a dud, but Jobs's keen eye for the customer's needs still paid off. The Xerox company had developed the technology for the computer mouse—a technology that Jobs had acquired for Apple in 1979. Jobs saw the mouse as the future of computing. "Within 10 minutes...it was clear to me that all computers would work this way someday," he later said.

Jobs applied the mouse technology, along with its graphical interface (which consisted of clickable icons), on the Apple Lisa (reportedly named for the daughter that Jobs had abandoned). He later also used it on the Macintosh (Mac).

Beginning in 1981, Jobs threw all his attention toward developing the Mac. He hoped that the Mac would reestablish the Apple name and erase memories of the flawed Apple III. It had the elegance that Jobs wanted in an Apple computer. Its graphical interface allowed for an ease of use and style that no other home computer on the market could match. Jobs remembered the calligraphy classes he'd attended and added a wealth of fancy fonts to the Mac. When it was finally complete, Jobs wanted to introduce it with a bang. So he bought advertising time during the 1984 Super Bowl. Apple's over-the-top, futuristic ad showed a society based on the novel *1984* by George Orwell. People in the society are shown as powerless workers in drab and lifeless surroundings. A single runner charges toward a large screen and throws a hammer into it, shattering it and freeing people from their bondage. Jobs was trying to show that the Mac would free society from a future ruled by dull business-based computers. The ad certainly got people talking. But in the end, many consumers gave the Mac the cold shoulder. The computer simply didn't have enough software to make it worth buying.

Apple was struggling. Sales were down. Computer innovator Bill Gates and his company, Microsoft, had run with the idea of a user-friendly graphical interface in a new operating system called Windows, stealing much of Apple's thunder. Furthermore, Jobs's erratic management style left worker morale at an all-time low, and he was constantly clashing with Apple CEO John Sculley. In April 1985, Sculley—whom Jobs had hired—convinced Apple's board to strip Jobs of his management duties. For all intents and purposes, Jobs had lost control of the company he'd created. It was not a situation Jobs could tolerate. In September he announced that he was cutting all ties to the company he'd created less than a decade before.

Jobs with John Sculley, the 1980s-era Apple CEO who eventually lost faith in Jobs's management style

The Next Big Thing?

Jobs wasn't about to just disappear. He still had a vision, and he was still driven to change the world of technology. Jobs sold off much of his share in Apple and poured it into his new company, NeXT. NeXT was in many ways the opposite of Apple. The computer system that this company built was designed for high-end business and education users. But its price tag, approaching $10,000, drove away most potential customers. After selling fewer than fifty thousand units, NeXT refocused on creating software.

Jobs with the first NeXT product in 1988

NeXT wasn't Jobs's only new project, however. He'd also bought a small special effects studio from *Star Wars* creator George Lucas. Jobs renamed the studio Pixar. He hoped it would give him a way to design new graphics hardware. But hardware turned out to be a dead end. Where Pixar really excelled was in animation. The studio produced a short film, *Tin Toy*, which won the 1988 Academy Award for animated short films—the first computer-generated film to do so.

Meanwhile, Jobs's personal life was changing. In 1990 he met business student Laurene Powell while giving a lecture at Stanford University in California. As Jobs was leaving the university, he couldn't get her out of his mind. He later recalled thinking, "If this is my last day on Earth, would I rather spend it in a business meeting or with this woman?" He made up his mind, turned around, and asked her out. A year later, the two were married. They would go on to have three children—Reed, Erin, and Eve.

Jobs and his wife, Laurene Powell, in 2005

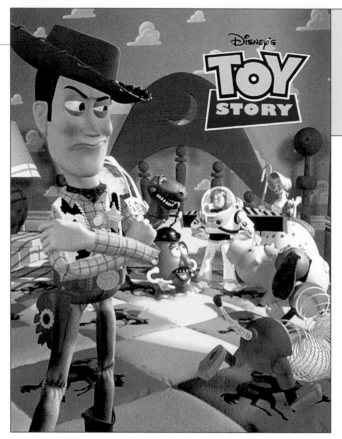

Woody, the lead character in *Toy Story,* stands in the foreground in this poster advertising the film.

In the early 1990s, the media giant Disney contracted Pixar to create several animated films. The deal launched a period of Jobs's life that he called one of his most creative. Pixar's first full-length film, *Toy Story*, was released in 1995. It was a hit. The film cost about $30 million to make but went on to gross more than $350 million worldwide. And that was only the beginning for Pixar. After Jobs sold the company to Disney for $7.4 billion in 1996, the studio cranked out hit after hit, including *A Bug's Life* (1998), *Toy Story 2* (1999), *Monsters, Inc.* (2001), and *Finding Nemo* (2003).

While Jobs was thriving, Apple was in deep trouble. The company was in danger of running out of money. In 1996 Apple bought NeXT for $430 million. Apple believed that the NeXT software could serve as the basis of a new Mac operating system. And the deal came with a bonus: Jobs would return to the company he had built two decades before, eventually to take over as CEO.

It proved to be exactly what both Apple and Jobs needed. The NeXT software would provide the footprint for every Apple product over the next decade and a half. And a more mature and business-savvy Jobs was ready to lead Apple to new heights. "The way we're going to survive," Jobs told an interviewer, "is to innovate our way out of this."

iDeas Man

In Apple, Jobs found a company with little direction. He wasted little time making his mark. Jobs pushed for the development of the Internet Macintosh—later dubbed the iMac. Jobs focused on a user-friendly and appealing product. The iMac, released in 1998, quickly became known for its brightly colored, see-through cases. It was an all-in-one machine, combining computer and monitor in a single unit. The design was a hit, especially with college students and other young people. As usual, Jobs wasn't afraid to take chances. He chose not to include a floppy disk drive on the iMac. The decision horrified some. Computers had always had floppy drives. But it proved wise. By the late 1990s, the floppy disk was all but dead, replaced by the CD-ROM.

Jobs speaks about the first-generation iPod as a giant image of the device looms behind him.

The iMac was a hit, and much-needed cash once again poured into Apple. But Jobs wasn't done there. By 2001 Internet rumors were flying about a new, secret Apple product soon to be released. That device was the iPod. Jobs and Apple didn't invent the digital music player. Such players had been around—and largely ignored—for several years. But Jobs did what no one else had done before: he made the idea cool. Before long, the iPod was the must-have tech item of the day. Sales of the little music player soared, and suddenly Apple was more than just a computer maker. Apple was branching out, and the brand itself was gaining its own measure of cool.

Jobs saw a bigger opportunity with the iPod. The market for digital music was in a state of disarray. The music industry couldn't seem to find a way to make a profit on music downloads. Frustrated customers often turned to pirated (illegally downloaded) music. So in 2003, Jobs and Apple launched the iTunes Store. The store offered easy and affordable music downloads. Suddenly, buying and downloading music seemed like a breeze. The iTunes service became yet another cash cow for Apple, and the company's stock soared. As the iPod evolved—allowing users to watch videos, play games, and more on the device—so too did iTunes. Before long, yearly profits from iTunes alone were in the billions. Devoted Apple fans who believed Jobs could do no wrong gave him the nickname iGod.

Jobs tells a crowd all about iTunes at the 2004 launch of the music service in Europe.

Apple was doing better than ever. But despite his immortal-sounding nickname, all was not well for Jobs. In 2003 his doctors found a growth on his pancreas. It was cancer. Although treatable, pancreatic cancer is one of the deadliest of cancers. Jobs at first resisted standard treatment. He tried alternative forms of therapy, including diet, to control the cancer. But when that failed, he turned to modern medicine and a liver transplant. Jobs made his condition public in 2004, declaring himself healed (although that was far from the truth).

In a June 2005 commencement speech given before Stanford graduates, Jobs offered a glimpse at the new perspective his illness had given him. "Remembering that you are going to die is the best way I know to avoid the trap of thinking you have something to lose," he told the graduates. "You are already naked. There is no reason not to follow your heart."

Jobs followed his heart by cranking out one successful product after the next. The iPhone debuted to an almost cultlike following in 2007. People waited in line for days just in the hopes of snagging one upon release. Its easy-to-use, elegant interface set a new standard for smartphones, and soon thousands of applications—or apps—were available for download. Apple, of course, was happy to sell customers all the apps they wanted in the new App Store—modeled after the successful iTunes.

And the hits kept coming. Jobs next turned his attention to the tablet computer. To some, it seemed like a rare misstep. Tablets had never interested consumers

Jobs shows off Apple's first iPhone to an enthusiastic audience.

in the past. But Jobs was ready to change that. He borrowed the simple, icon-based interface of the iPhone and imported it to a tablet—the iPad. The iPad debuted in 2010. Many in the computer industry expected it to flop. It was just a giant iPhone but without a phone, they argued. But once again, Jobs proved that he knew

A consumer lifts a boxed iPad off the shelf at an Apple Store.

how to sell people something they hadn't even known they needed. Apple sold more than 15 million iPads in the first year, and the industry was turned on its ear. Suddenly everyone seemed to want an iPad, and competitors rushed to produce iPad knockoffs. It was the perfect example of what made Jobs such a genius. He could take a product that nobody had wanted before and turn it into one that suddenly everyone *had* to have and competitors *had* to copy. It seemed that Jobs could do no wrong.

The Passing of a Legend

Rumors about Jobs's health had begun to swirl again. He appeared thin—even gaunt. He did his best to keep it quiet, but he was slowly losing his battle with cancer. The change in his appearance was startling to many fans—and Apple shareholders. Jobs claimed that he just had a common bug, but he wasn't really fooling anyone.

Jobs, battling late-stage cancer in June 2011, appears before a crowd in his familiar black turtleneck topped with a cashmere sweater. He is speaking passionately about iCloud—Apple's service for online content storage.

The day that Apple fans and shareholders had dreaded finally came in August 2011. Jobs announced that he was stepping down as the company's CEO. "I have always said that if there ever came a day when I could no longer meet my duties and expectations as Apple's CEO, I would be the first to let you know," Jobs said in a letter. "Unfortunately, that day has come."

Jobs knew that he was dying. He spent his final weeks with his family and friends. He worked with author Walter Isaacson on finalizing his biography, *Steve Jobs*. The book was important to Jobs because he wanted to be sure his children could better know and understand him.

Walter Isaacson's biography of Jobs sold about 379,000 print copies in the first week it went on sale. In addition, many readers downloaded the book through iBooks and Amazon.

Written tributes to Jobs cover the front of the San Francisco Apple Store in October 2011.

On October 4, 2011, in his Palo Alto, California, home, Steve Jobs lost consciousness due to complications from his cancer. He died the following day. Rarely has the death of an entrepreneur so affected the world. Tributes poured in from around the globe. Jobs was laid to rest at a small private funeral on October 7. On October 16, a larger, invitation-only memorial was held at Stanford University. Many fans held vigils of their own, often in or outside Apple stores.

President Barack Obama was among the many to pay tribute to Jobs. As Obama put it, "Steve was among the greatest of American innovators—brave enough to think differently, bold enough to believe he could change the world, and talented enough to do it. . . . The world has lost a visionary."

Important Dates

1955   Steven Paul Jobs is born on February 24 in San Francisco, California, and is adopted by Paul and Clara Jobs.

1970   Jobs meets Steve Wozniak while working at Hewlett-Packard.

1972   Jobs graduates from high school and attends Reed College in Portland, Oregon.

1973   He drops out of Reed College but continues sitting in on classes.

1974   He takes a job designing video games for Atari. He takes a spiritual journey to India.

1976   He and Wozniak start Apple and sell Wozniak's Apple I computer.

1977   Jobs and Wozniak unveil the Apple II. Sales soar, and Apple begins to make big profits.

1978   Chrisann Brennan gives birth to Jobs's daughter Lisa.

1979	Jobs secures the rights to use the graphical interface and mouse technology developed by the Xerox company.
1980	Apple goes public. Its stock climbs from $22 to $29 in a single day.
1984	The Mac is released, but sales are disappointing.
1985	Jobs leaves Apple after being stripped of his management duties. He starts a new company, NeXT.
1986	He buys a special effects company from George Lucas and names it Pixar.
1988	Pixar's short animated film, *Tin Toy*, wins an Academy Award.
1991	Jobs marries Laurene Powell.
1995	Pixar releases *Toy Story*, which goes on to gross more than $350 million worldwide.

1996	Jobs sells Pixar to Disney for $7.4 billion. Apple buys NeXT, and Jobs returns to Apple as CEO.
1998	Apple releases the iMac.
2001	Apple releases the iPod.
2003	Apple launches the iTunes Store, for the first time making music downloads easy and affordable. Jobs discovers that he has pancreatic cancer.
2007	Apple releases the iPhone.
2010	Apple releases the iPad, setting off a new trend in personal computing.
2011	Apple launches iCloud, an online storage service for content such as music, photos, apps, and documents. In August, Jobs steps down as CEO of Apple. He dies on October 5 from complications of cancer.

Source Notes

8 Brad Stone, "With iPad Tablet, Apple Blurs the Line between Devices," *New York Times*, January 27, 2010, http://www.nytimes.com/2010/01/28/technology/companies/28apple.html (November 4, 2011).

10 Walter Isaacson, *Steve Jobs* (New York : Simon & Schuster, 2011), 28.

10 *Macleans*, "Thinking Different," October 2011, 36.

12 Isaacson, *Steve Jobs*, 31.

13 Ibid., 37.

14 Ibid., 31.

15 Ibid., 45.

16 Rupert Neate, "Steve Wozniak Interview: Iconic Co-founder on the iPod, iPhone, and Future for Apple," *Telegraph*, October 6, 2008, http://www.telegraph.co.uk/finance/newsby-sector/mediatechnologyandtelecoms/3145691/Steve-Wozniak-interview-iconic-co-founder-on-the-iPod-iPhone-and-future-for-Apple.html (October 27, 2011).

22 Isaacson, *Steve Jobs*, 58.

23 Ibid., 59.

24 Ibid., 63.

25 Harry McCracken, "Steve Jobs, 1955–2011: Mourning Technology's Great Reinventor," *Time*, October 5, 2011, http://www.time.com/time/business/article/0,8599,2096251-2,00.html (November 2, 2011).

29 *Macleans*, "Thinking Different," 40–41.

31 McCracken, "Steve Jobs."

34 *Macleans*, "Thinking Different," 42.

38 David Strietfeld, "Jobs Steps Down at Apple, Saying He Can't Meet Duties," *New York Times*, August 12, 2011, http://www.nytimes.com/2011/08/25/technology/jobs-stepping-down-as-chief-of-apple.html?pagewanted=all (November 4, 2011).

39 Lauren Effron, "President Obama, Bill Gates, Mark Zuckerberg, Others React to Steve Jobs' Death," *ABC News*, October 5, 2011, http://abcnews.go.com/Technology/reaction-steve-jobs-death/story?id=14678187#.TrQMHPRV1QA (November 4, 2011).

Selected Bibliography

Curley, Robert, ed. *The 100 Most Influential Inventors of All Time.* New York: Britannica Educational Pub., 2010.

Isaacson, Walter. *Steve Jobs.* New York: Simon & Schuster, 2011. e-book.

Kahney, Leander. *Inside Steve's Brain.* New York: Penguin, 2008.

Macleans. "Thinking Different." October 2011, 32–45.

McCracken, Harry. "Steve Jobs, 1955–2011: Mourning Technology's Great Reinventor," *Time,* October 5, 2011. http://www.time.com/time/business/article/0,8599,2096251-1,00.html

Young, Jeffrey S. *iCon: Steve Jobs, the Greatest Second Act in the History of Business.* Hoboken, NJ: Wiley, 2005.

Further Reading

Books

DK Publishing. *Computer*. New York: DK, 2011.

Gillam, Scott. *Steve Jobs: Apple & iPod Wizard*. Edina, MN: Abdo, 2008.

Imbimbo, Anthony. *Steve Jobs: The Brilliant Mind behind Apple*. Pleasantville, NY: Gareth Stevens, 2009.

Lesinski, Jeanne M. *Bill Gates: Entrepreneur and Philanthropist*. Minneapolis: Twenty-First Century Books, 2009.

Sheen, Barbara. *Steve Jobs*. Detroit: Lucent Books, 2010.

Venezia, Mike. *Steve Jobs & Steve Wozniak: Geek Heroes Who Put the Personal in Computers*. New York: Children's Press, 2010.

Websites

Apple
http://www.apple.com
Apple's home page is loaded with information on all Apple products. It also includes a page where fans can leave tributes to Steve Jobs (http://www.apple.com/stevejobs).

The Apple Museum
http://www.theapplemuseum.com
Take a trip back in time as you surf this page devoted to past Apple products. Learn more about the famous Apple II, the early Mac, and even failed products such as the Apple III and the Apple Lisa. The site also includes a detailed Steve Jobs bio.

Biography.com—Steve Jobs
   http://www.biography.com/people/steve-jobs-9354805
   This short biography touches on the highlights of Steve Jobs's
   personal and professional life. The site includes photos and a
   memorial video.

Macworld
   http://www.macworld.com
   Macworld magazine is devoted to all things Apple, from the
   Macintosh computer to the iPhone and the iPad. Read about
   upcoming Apple products and software, read reviews, and see
   photos and videos of Apple products at work.

Pixar Animation Studios
   http://www.pixar.com
   Check out the site of Pixar. Jobs helped turn this company
   into the most successful animation studio in the world before
   he sold it to Disney in 1996. Learn more about how Pixar
   works and read about its many animated films.

Steve Jobs—Forbes
   http://www.forbes.com/profile/steve-jobs
   If you're interested in learning more about Steve Jobs the
   businessman, this page is for you. Jobs's profile in *Forbes*
   magazine is loaded with business info on Jobs and the impact
   he made on Apple and the computer industry.

Index